We Went On
Folding Laundry

**Reflections that comfort in the fresh season of grief,
and when continuing on as seasons come and go,
with pages for personal reflection**

Reflections on . . .

Life and its passing, *Death,* **and the process of grief,**

and

Eternal Life,

the joyful future promised to Christians

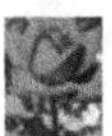

By Audrey Marie Hessler

Library of Congress Cataloging-in-Publication Date
Hessler, Audrey Marie
        Grief: death / poetry/ Christianity
ISBN-13: 978-1481168816
ISBN-10: 1481168819

1. Grief—Christianity 2. Poetry 3. Wisdom
Prose and poetry by Audrey Marie Hessler
*All Rights Reserved

All references to the Bible are from the authorized King James Version.

Dedication

To all who have experienced the season of

a time to weep . . . a time to mourn . . .

and *continue on* with life.

For Ellen
Crosses on the Road

I have felt the mournful sorrow of those who set
Flowers with crosses on the road. "Explain to me,

Lord, help me understand this painful mystery."
But there is no answer, no explaining of it.

Yet, the One who carried the cross whispers softly,
"My child, what breaks the heart of thee, breaks the heart of me."

Blessed are they that mourn for they shall be comforted.

Matthew 5:4

Contents

Introduction

Part I: *Reflections on Life and Its Passing* 9-24

With My Praying Hands
Soon
Valley of the Shadow
Valley of the Shadow, Author's Reflection
It's the Game of Life
It Came To Pass
Our Life's Day
Personal Reflection

Part II: *Death* 25-40

Gone Home
A Homesick Traveler
And So, We Say, Goodbye
And So, We Say, Goodbye, Author's Reflection
A Little Dog's Bark, The Passing of Amy's Grandfather
God is Here and There
Personal Reflection

Part III: *The Process of Grief—Personal* 41-58

We Went on Folding Laundry
I'm Glad There's a Heaven
Goodbye, Loved One
Treasures in Heaven
Love is the Warrior Brave
Birds of a Feather
I Wish
I Wish, Author's Reflection
Personal Reflection

Part IV: *The Process of Grief—Collective* 59-82

The Memory Continues
Remembering Our Lady of Angels School Fire
A Fireman's Daughter
Remembering Firemen and the Heroes of 9-11
A Fireman's Daughter, Author's Reflection
The Empty Desk
Remembering Andy and a Special Sixth Grade Class
Bend Your Knee, Say a Prayer
Remembering LCpl. James Bray Stack and our sacrificial military men and women
Heaven Knew This Man!
Remembering President Ronald Reagan
Personal Reflection

Part V: *Eternal Life* 83-94

When All of Heaven Rejoices
When All of Heaven Rejoices, Author's Reflection

Contents

Part V: *Eternal Life* *continued*................................. *83-94*
Then Comes the Day of Singing!
The Painting of Paradise

Author's Afterword *About the Dedication* *97*

A Note on the Personal Reflection pages . . .

At the end of each of the five topical sections in this book are *Personal*
Reflection **pages**. If you wish, use these pages to write your own poem,
memories, or thoughts. Share it with family members or friends, or have
them write their own, too. Any way you choose to use these pages, even if
you leave them blank and you just pause to mentally reflect at those pages,
may it be another helpful tool on your journey of processing grief.

Introduction

Though it was many years ago, it is still etched in my heart and mind, the summer my younger brother was found dead. He died in his sleep after a series of tumultuous years. Ten years earlier his fragile teenage voice told me over the phone that my mother was dying. Now everyone said he had peace because he was with his mother. But I had no peace about his death.

When the phone call came this time, it was my older brother, who also now is with the Lord, telling me the news. I had just returned home from a weekend getaway. Upon arriving at my home, I gathered my clothes from the weekend trip and started a load of laundry.

The washing machine hummed along, and when it finished I put the clothes in the dryer. I then sat on the sofa, planning to pray through a list of prayers. My first prayer on my list was for my younger brother. I asked God, *"Is this the right prayer for Johnny?"* At the moment of my questioning, the phone rang . . .

The phone call was to tell me of my brother's death.

And so began the process of grief. It's not a neat process that fits exactly into these compartments, but I did experience to varying degrees: denial, anger, bargaining, depression, and then finally with the help of the Lord, acceptance.

It was a week after that phone call when I walked downstairs to the laundry room to find my clothes still sitting in the dryer. I had to go back to that dryer that represented the point at which life had abruptly halted. And I had to go through the grief process, going on with everyday life. I went on folding laundry.

The Bible says that it is *appointed unto a man once to die.* (Hebrew 9:27) Death is inevitable, and we must therefore deal with it as part of the human condition. Today God sets before us life and death. When given the opportunity to make a choice, God says that we are to *choose life.* (Deut. 30:19)

This does not mean that people necessarily think to take their life, but that since grief is hard there is a need to choose to go on with life and *live it.* Today God sets before us life and death—and we are to *choose life.* We can do this even in times of grief, if we rest in God's goodness, even when we don't have every answer—or even any answers at all. And we can do this, though it may be a process, because we can rest in *this answer*—God is love and loves our loved ones and us. Someday, He will wipe away every tear. And *there will be no more sorrow and no more death.* (Rev. 21:4)

All who grieve know there is a point at which life stops—and the grief begins. Whether we were doing laundry at that moment or not, we all must face going back to doing everyday tasks after the loss of our loved ones. Let this book bring a measure of comfort to you as you continue on in that process. Or, use this book to help others who grieve. The Lord has asked us to *comfort those who weep.* (Is. 40:1)

The process of grief is a life long journey. It enters our lives and recedes, like waves of the sea, grief rushes in and out on the shoreline of our lives. Grief is complex. And, though we share many similarities with others who grieve, we also each express our grief uniquely.

Wherever you are on your journey, let Christ come alongside you *to comfort you,* as He, too, has grieved, *to strengthen you,* as He has overcome death, and *to heal you,* as He is the Great Physician, so you can *continue on* doing the work you have been placed here to do.

We went on folding laundry. That's what love would do.

Audrey Marie Hessler

Part I

Reflections on Life and Its Passing

To everything there is a season

Eccl. 3:1a

With My Praying Hands

I leave you now—for now—my loved one,
This day, knowing we must part.
And I say this bittersweet goodbye to you,
Thinking of how it all did start.

You brought to my world, this world, a gift,
A gift that only you could give—
The gift was your precious life,
The life only you could live.

A unique special someone,
A star shining bright, twinkling in the night,
You were shining among the many,
But for me, for us—a very special light.

So I wave my hand goodbye to you
Saying, We will meet again.
And I hear echo back so softly,
We will meet again. Amen

Always—now and forever—I will know
How much we truly cared,
And with my praying hands I'll hold
The breath of life we shared.

We Went On Folding Laundry

Soon

Soon the summer came a callin'
Soon after a blissful new birth.
Soon all the fields flowed with flowers.
Soon was green the leaves of God's earth.

Soon all the beauty was changin'.
Soon the colors were bright and deep.
Soon came leaves of gold and fall's frost.
Soon all wearied ready to sleep.

Soon tired leaves fell to the ground.
Soon the trees were quiet and bare.
Soon all was the white of winter.
Soon soft silence was everywhere.

Soon small buds of leaves were burstin'.
Soon the fields were sweet with clover.
Soon there was the joyful springtime.
Soon the time to grieve was over.

Valley of the Shadow *(p.1 of 2)*

Early morning

a new soft light begins to shimmer

Across spring green grass where a mother blue jay

Teaches her baby to fly amidst shadows that play.

Branches sway of the old willow. Move quicker.

Quicker,

Nudges the mother, as the baby slow

Lands by a tree, shadows of light glint on the blue

Of the determined mother, proud of her fledgling, too.

Wings flap and flutter to fly, stop then go.

Go.

And the children happy in the yard, run, run, run.

The light now grows strong to bright golden midday

Sun as the winds blow soft, shadows dance every way.

Dance every way as children play. Laughter and fun.

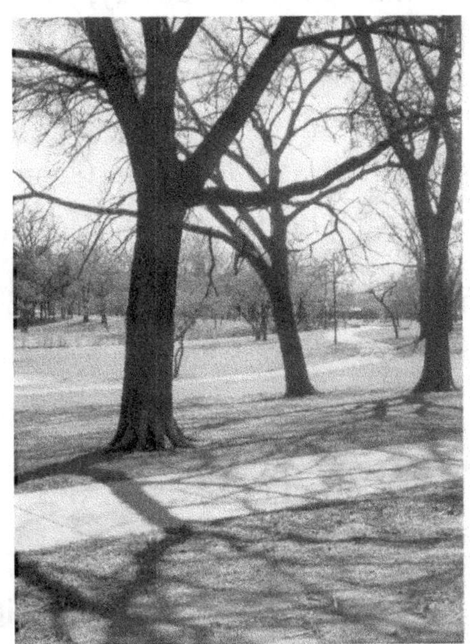

Fun and play

In the yard all day 'til the dinner hour's

Here, and Father with the hose walks and waters all around.

The sun in the west seems to be falling to the ground

As the shadows grow long on watered grass and flowers.

Flowers are picked

By children who come out for the end

Of evening sun and run to grandmother to give her one,

A pretty flower. She smiles and then the children run

Between shadows of the setting sun, and a kiss they send.

We Went On Folding Laundry

Valley of the Shadow *(p.2 of 2)*

Send a kiss

As they wave good night. Only a little light

Remains amidst the valley of shadow everywhere.

Shadows cover the yard where children played without care

Amidst shadows all day, now sleeping safe in the night.

Night descends.

Walking through the last long shadow

As night falls where the shadows flickered all day.

I fear no evil, for Thou art with me all the way,

Though I walk through the valley of the shadow.

Shadow of death.

I will fear no evil.

For Thou art with me, and I with Thee.

Surely goodness and mercy follow me.

I will dwell in the house of the Lord forever.

> *"Shadow of death.*
> *I will fear no evil.*
> *For Thou art with me,*
> *and I with Thee."*

Valley of the Shadow—Author's Reflection

Shadows are everywhere. Since the day of our birth, through all the years of our life, we have moved and walked and played and worked within shadows. They are everywhere, and they are harmless. And so is the *shadow of death* for those who are in Christ Jesus. How many times have we heard the twenty-third Psalm and John 3:16? Put them together and what do you have but the complete answer as to why the *shadow of death* is harmless, without sting. John 3:16 says: *For God so loved the world that He gave his only begotten son, that whosoever believes in him should not perish, but have everlasting life.* Psalm 23: *I will fear no evil for thou art with me.* Who is with me that *I will fear no evil, and I will fear no shadow of death?* The Son, Jesus, that died for us to have everlasting life.

"Walking through the last long shadow
I fear no evil, for Thou art with me all the way,
Though I walk through the valley of the shadow."

They that dwell in the land of the shadow of death,
upon them hath the light shined.
Isaiah 9:2-7b

Yea, though I walk through the valley of the shadow of death,
I will fear no evil, for thou art with me.
Psalm 23:4a

It's the Game of Life *(p.1 of 3)*

I love baseball.

I love to cheer on the players with zest.

To pitch and bat, to hit, run, slide, and do their best.

I love to be in the crowd with anticipation,

Hearing sung the sweet anthem of our nation;

And then to hear the words shouted: "Play ball!"

I love it all!

I love baseball.

I love to see the players run onto the field.

And the pitcher on the mound who will wield

The ball at speeds that will astound

In ways that will confound;

He winds up—the pitch—a strike! It's a curve ball.

I love it all!

I love baseball.

I love to hear the crack of the bat hitting the ball,

And watch wondering whether into the glove it will fall.

As the players run the bases

All the fans watch with eager faces.

And all sigh together when it's caught—a fly ball.

I love it all!

I love baseball.

When the starting lineup's at the bat

There's nothing more exciting or hopeful than that.

A swing—a hit— a double could be on the way.

A triple? A home run would make our day.

> *"Wherefore seeing we also are compassed about with so great a cloud of witnesses . . .*

The umpire makes the call—it's a foul ball.

I love it all!

I love baseball.

When a player on your team catches a high pop up,

Or a ground ball is stopped by the short stop;

The other team is trying to fill the bases,

But there's a sad look on their faces—

There's a double play in two quick throws of the ball.

I love it all!

I love baseball.

The sounds, the smells, the feeling in the air.

"Peanuts!" "Popcorn!" The vendors sell their ware.

The seventh inning stretch—two more innings to play.

Hopes are for a pennant? The World Series? We can pray.

For today—"Safe!" or "Out!" We listen to each call.

I love it all!

I love baseball.

The catcher signals to the pitcher on the mound.

Someone tries to steal—quick the ball goes round.

The ball whirs to second then first in a quick bout.

It's the ninth; now we need extra innings—he is out!

Who is going to win this game of ball?

I love it all!

I love baseball.

> *. . . let us run with*
> *patience the race*
> *that is set before.*
> *Looking unto Jesus*
> *the author and*
> *finisher of*
> *our faith."*
> *Hebrews 12; 1a, 2b*

We Went On Folding Laundry

It's the Game of Life *(p.3 of 3)*

Faith is part of every play; the manager signals the one at bat

For a hit—bases are loaded—there's *hope* for more than that!

A grand slam! "It's out of the park!" you'd *love* to hear,

So the crowd is to their feet ready to cheer,

And… "It's outta here!" You no longer see the ball!

I love it all!

I love baseball.

It's the game of life we all love and play.

We're watched by a crowd, as we play for our team each day.

One day, you're team's winning, you hit high and far away,

Then you're roundin' the bases sliding into home today.

And the Umpire of All says, "Safe!" Safe at home is the call.

I love it all!

I love baseball.

I love it all!

> ***"Then you're roundin' the bases sliding into home today.***
> ***And the Umpire of All says, 'Safe!'***
> ***Safe at home is the call."***

It Came To Pass

It passes like a light mist this day,
Like a night dream won't stay.
It passes like a sailing ship from the bay,
Like a spring flower's fragrance in May.
It passes away.

It passes like waves on the sand,
Like a small child holding your hand.
It passes like deer across the woodland,
Like a summer parade with a band.
It passes away.

It passes like soft winds through trees,
Like a refreshing cool breeze.
It passes like a heartbeat with ease.
Like fall and twirling leaves.
It passes away.

It passes like birds flying overhead,
Like a simple hello that was said.
It passes like sweet sleep in the bed,
Like a swift winter sled.
It passes away.

It passes like you passed away,
Like I, too, cannot stay.
It came to pass as God did say,
Like night and dawn of day.
It passes away.

We Went On Folding Laundry

Our Life's Day

I like the pale gold light that begins
a long sweet summer day.

I like the sound of children playing
as an evening quietly gives way.

I like talking with a friend and
the feeling of a gentle fall breeze.

I like the crisp shuffle at my feet
of golden autumn leaves.

I like to see the soft white blanket
of an early morning winter snow.

I like to see the footprints of animals,
wondering where they go.

I like cards from loved ones and the
cold winter coming to an end.

I like that God commands the world,
and with love sends spring again.

I like the beauty of the tulip blooming,
and the birds returning from far away.

I like the pale gold light that begins—
and ends our life's day.

Personal Reflection

We Went On Folding Laundry

Personal Reflection

Part II

Death

A time to be born, and a time to die
Eccl. 3:2

For if we believe that Jesus died and rose again,
even so them also which sleep in Jesus will God bring with him.
I Thessalonians 4:14

Gone Home

I heard that you had gone away.
Gone home—that is what I had heard.
I knew that I'd really miss you
From the moment I got the word.

You hear that some have gone to school.
You hear that some have gone to war.
But it seems that when someone has
Gone home, you miss 'em even more.

I guess there's a special missing
That is different for each place.
But there's one good thing about this—
When I go home, I'll see your face.

I may not go to school again.
I may never go off to war.
But someday I'll go home and there
You'll be to greet me at the door.

A Homesick Traveler *(p.1 of 2)*

Anywhere I wander, anywhere I roam,

I am on a journey heading toward my home.

Such a forlorn traveler, wanting to go home.

I'm a lonely foreigner waiting to go home,

Anywhere I wander, anywhere I roam.

Oh, how I'm wanting to be with loved ones again.

I would like to see them waving 'round the bend.

I'm a lonesome traveler wanting to go home.

Anywhere I wander, anywhere I roam,

I have been walking long hard roads with tears.

I have waited longingly in the lonesome years.

I'm a lonely foreigner waiting to go home,

Anywhere I wander, anywhere I roam.

There's a longing, hoping part of me,

Says, I'm not home yet, but someday I will be.

I'm a lonesome traveler wanting to go home.

Anywhere I wander, anywhere I roam,

Do you know I miss you and your embrace?

How I long to see you and look into your face.

I'm a lonely foreigner waiting to go home,

Anywhere I wander, anywhere I roam.

You are in my heart always, every place,

But how I long, how I long to see your face.

I'm a lonesome traveler wanting to go home.

Anywhere I wander, anywhere I roam,

Such a tired traveler, such a load of care.

Lord, help me carry this. I know You are there.

I'm a lonely foreigner waiting to go home,

Anywhere I wander, anywhere I roam.

Sometimes skies are sunny; sometimes they're blue.

But there is no resting, 'til I rest with You.

I'm a lonesome traveler wanting to go home.

Anywhere I wander, anywhere I roam,

I hear Your promise: You prepared a place for me.

Love will be found faithful on this journey.

I'm a lonely foreigner waiting to go home,

Anywhere I wander, anywhere I roam.

Love will lead me home. Lead me home safely.

Love will lead me home. Love will lead me.

I'm a lonesome traveler wanting to go home.

Anywhere I wander, anywhere I roam,

I'm looking farther up the road ahead.

Father, are those angels standing 'round my bed?

I'm a lonely foreigner waiting to go home,

Anywhere I wander, anywhere I roam.

Now I know I'm waiting for those words You'll say.

Now I hear You saying, "Come home, Child, today."

I'm a homesick traveler wanting to go home.

Anywhere I wander, anywhere I roam,

Now I know it's true—Love will lead me home.

> *"Anywhere I wander, anywhere I roam, Now I know it's true—Love will lead me home."*

We Went On Folding Laundry

And So, We Say, Goodbye (p.1 of 2)

And so, we say, goodbye. Oh, goodbye. Goodbye.

We knew, we knew this time would come,

But I'm grieving this goodbye. I'm not the only one.

Please forgive me if I cry; hearing goodbye, I cry.

No, I'm not the only one grieving, missing you.

We rehearse the last words we each had to say.

We remember our last moments before today.

I'm not the only one missing you—so many do.

And we all knew our paths would someday part.

We know God plans, plans our lives that way

For a season—but today seemed not the day,

No, or the way. It seems too soon we are apart.

Too soon from our tiny, tiny point of view.

We struggle with the grand, majestic mystery.

Our lives intertwined have their own destiny.

To your Heavenly view, oh God, our minds renew.

For a while we shared as travelers the road of life,

And we remember shared smiles and shared sorrow,

And hope shared, oh the hope shared for tomorrow.

And now your journey ends, set free from the strife.

We rejoice in your life, but tears roll down our face.

We let you go to the heavenly home that awaits you,

A home your brothers and sisters also long to go to.

As one of the runners, you finished well your race.

> *"We struggle with the grand, majestic mystery.*
> *Our lives intertwined have their own destiny."*

And so, we say, goodbye. Oh, goodbye. Goodbye.

Oh, I'm glad there is good in this difficult word,

Because the word now is so hard, hard to be heard.

But there is good in goodbye, even though we cry.

Joy will eclipse death's shadow and searing sorrow

Though our paths separate, it's for a short while.

In a tomorrow, face to face we'll meet and smile.

And we say goodbye, not forever, no, but for now.

So the final word is, as a tear rolls from our eye,

Is the word that makes us sad, brings us comfort too—

Goodbye means God be with ye, and God is with you,

And you are with God, and so, we say, goodbye.

> *"Goodbye means God be with ye, and God is with you,*
>
> *And you are with God, and so, we say, goodbye."*

We Went On Folding Laundry

And So, We Say, Goodbye—Author's Reflection

We say goodbye so many times during our lifetime—every day when we leave our home, or work, or school—but when it is that "final" goodbye, we experience varying levels of sadness and grief. However, no matter what our level of grief, from the slight ache to the deepest raw pain, we have God's promise, and what a magnificent promise it is: *That whosoever believes in Him…has eternal life.* This is why Christ died that we might have life. And so our confidence is, as the poem says: "Though our paths separate, it's for a short while. In a tomorrow, face to face we'll meet and smile."

He will swallow up death in victory;
and the Lord God will wipe away tears from off all faces.
Isaiah 25:8

That whosoever believes in Him should not perish,
but have eternal life.
For God so loved the world
that he gave
his only begotten son
that whosoever believes in him should not perish,
but have everlasting life.
John 3:15-16

A Little Dog's Bark
The Passing of Amy's Grandfather

Young and fair in nature among the lasses,

A gentle girl with long tresses and glasses

Spoke one day about this story tenderly,

Gathered with her grandfather was her family.

They were with him for his last days to be near.

And as they sat by his side, they did hear

Their little dog yap, yapping at a corner space.

And the old grandpa pointed to that very place.

He said, "Look! An angel has come to take me."

Then the grandfather smiled and left peacefully.

As the white clouds silently above us passed by

It seemed we understood, the young girl and I.

Once angels were acknowledged with—Hark!

Now they are announced by a little dog's bark.

> *"Look!*
> *An angel has come*
> *to take me."*
> *Then the*
> *grandfather smiled*
> *and left*
> *peacefully."*

God is Here And There *(p.1 of 2)*

Within the worry.

In the flurry.

Against the flow.

And then to go

Where there is need.

Planting the seed

Of what is true.

Following through.

Not looking back.

Having no lack.

To love much more

Than ever before.

Not to fear—

God is here.

Through the trouble.

March on the double.

Facing pain.

Finding there's gain.

Hearing a call.

Calling to all.

To war we go

Against the foe.

A battle to fight.

Dark against light.

Losing then winning.

Dying is beginning.

Not to fear—

God is here.

> *"Losing then winning.*
> *Dying is beginning.*
> *Not to fear—*
> *God is here."*

God is Here And There

Amidst the trial

For a short while.

Suffering so.

Then letting go.

Singing a new song.

All pain is gone.

No more tears to cry.

Sorrow it will die.

Light is dark's defeat.

Victory is complete.

Keeping our eyes there.

The finish line is clear.

Not to fear—

God is here—and there.

> *"No more tears to cry.*
>
> *Sorrow it will die.*
>
> *Light is dark's defeat.*
>
> *Victory is complete."*

We Went On Folding Laundry

Personal Reflection

"Jesus said . . . I am the resurrection and the life:

he that believes in me, though he were dead

yet shall he live."

John 11:25

Personal Reflection

Part III

The Process of Grief— Personal

A time to break down . . . a time to weep

Eccl. 3:3,4a

We Went on Folding Laundry (p.1 of 2)

We went on folding laundry.
Thinking, it wasn't true that you were gone.

We went on folding laundry,
Thinking, hoping—something was wrong.

We went on folding laundry,
As if you had not gone away.

We went on folding laundry.
Folding the shirts and socks in their own way.

We went on folding laundry.
No! No, our hearts could not be glad!

We went on folding laundry.
We realized, yes, we realized—we were mad!

We went on folding laundry
Looking at clothes you used to wear.

We went on folding laundry.
What could we do—so you would still be here?

We went on folding laundry.
Then we felt we had no feelings; all we felt was bad.

We went on folding laundry
Slowly, knowing—we were very sad.

> *"So my spirit grows faint within me; my heart within me is dismayed . . . my soul thirsts for you like a parched land."*
> *Ps. 34: 4,6*

We Went On Folding Laundry

We Went on Folding Laundry *(p.2 of 2)*

We went on folding laundry
We'd fold each piece over, as if bending to pray.

We went on folding laundry
Each piece bent over in its own special way.

We went on folding laundry,
And softly, we would mention your name.

We went on folding laundry
We knew now—things would not be the same.

And sometimes we would talk about another time.
How it used to be that clothes were dried upon a line.
Clothes on a line on a warm summer day,
All the clothes together in the gentle breeze sway.
It was like—we were all together there.
I could see the bright colors and breathe the fresh air.
It seemed I saw a vision of a time gone by—
And yet it was a day to come seen through a teary eye.

We went on folding laundry.
We did what love would say to do.

We went on folding laundry.
We went on without you.

> *"We did what*
> *love would say*
> *to do . . .*
> *We went on*
> *without you."*

I'm Glad There's a Heaven

I'm glad there's a heaven;

That it's a blissful, beautiful place.

I'm glad there's a heaven

That exists beyond time and space.

I'm glad there's a heaven;

It's not just a sweet story that was told.

I'm glad there's a heaven,

A place where no one will grow old.

I'm glad there's a heaven

Where there is no more crying or pain.

I'm glad there's a heaven

Where all that was loss is now gain.

I'm glad there's a heaven

With golden streets; God is the sunlight.

I'm glad there's a heaven.

The darkness is gone; there is no night.

I'm glad there's a heaven;

That all I've ever heard is true.

Most of all, I'm glad there's a heaven

Because there I'll be with the Lord and you.

> *"I'm glad there's a heaven; It's not just a sweet story that was told."*

Goodbye, Loved One *(p.1 of 2)*

Goodbye, Loved One, it's your time.

They are opening for you heaven's gate.

Angels stretch their arms out toward you,

They smile, smile and patiently wait.

Goodbye, Loved One, I'll miss you!

Oh, I'll miss you, my dear friend.

I'm so glad we'll meet again.

This is not our true journey's end.

Goodbye, Loved One, understand.

Understand, and you must know,

We'll part for a while, and so we'll grieve.

Yes, we'll grieve to let you go.

"I'm so glad

we'll meet again.

This is not our true

journey's end."

But, goodbye, Loved One, trust and know,

Know, our hearts are rejoicing, too!

Yes, rejoicing, happy knowing

A heavenly mansion's home for you.

So, goodbye, Loved One, my dear one,

Our Loved One, so loved and dear,

You're free to leave the troubles

That earth holds here.

Goodbye, Loved One, head home.

Hear heaven's music start to play.

Let heaven have its way,

Its joyful welcoming day.

Goodbye, Loved One *(p.2 of 2)*

Goodbye, Loved One, with the Lord

With other loved ones now are you.

You've gone to our heavenly home,

As those in the family do.

Goodbye, Loved One, watch for loved ones here.

Stretch your arms toward us as the angels do.

Soon you'll welcome us home, too.

Someday in heaven with you.

Goodbye, Loved One, we love you.

Goodbye, Loved One, I love you.

> *"You've gone to our heavenly home,*
>
> *As those in the family do."*

We Went On Folding Laundry

Treasures in Heaven

We have these treasures in vessels of clay

For a brief moment these treasures are here.

In earthen vessels here for a short stay,

Then these treasures fly away—they disappear.

Oh, my treasure! Oh, treasure of my heart.

My priceless treasure! Where is my treasure?

Where? *Where your treasure is, so is your heart.*

Where is my heart? Did it leave me? *It's there—*

In heaven! There's the treasure of my heart;

For a while my treasure I cannot see.

They heard a whisper: It's time to depart.

Yes, my dear treasure though not here with me—

My heart's with you, my treasure, with you in

My heart, my treasure is with you—in heaven.

Love is the Warrior Brave *(p.1 of 2)*

Every heart that loves today

Across every wave tossed shore

Beats with my heart with love this day

Saying—I couldn't love you more.

I couldn't love you more.

Everything that could divide—

Distance, death, time and space,

Mountains, valleys, oceans wide—

There is no deep, high, far away place

That can keep love apart. There is no place!

Everyone who loves a sister, a brother,

A child, a friend, a husband, wife, father,

A mother, or any other—

This truth they will discover.

This truth they will uncover.

Love is the warrior brave—

Years have no value; they are naught—

Love goes beyond the grave.

The seeker seeking finds what is sought.

This is the truth Jesus taught.

Love is a ship with windblown sail

Sailing seas of space and time.

Love does not end, nor does it fail.

Carrying its cargo to the distant shoreline,

Love, its loved one, it will find.

We Went On Folding Laundry

Love is the Warrior Brave   *(p.2 of 2)*

Nothing separates us from the love of God.

Loved one, you lived and died in His embrace,

Safe in the arms of our Savior Lord.

Together then, some day we'll see His face.

Together then, we'll all embrace.

Through His saving grace,

We'll be together again; we'll be together where

We'll look into His love-filled face.

Together—then and there—

All will be made clear.

Till then, love sails on

Sailing seas of hope and anticipation

Seeing Love's full reception

On the shore at the glorious final destination.

Until then—love continues on.

Every heart that loves today

Across every earthly wave tossed shore

Beats with my heart with love this day

Saying—I couldn't love you more.

I'll see you on heaven's shore.

"Neither death,

nor life, nor angels,

nor principalities,

nor powers,

nor things present,

nor things to come . . .

shall be able to separate

us from the love of God,

which is in Christ Jesus

our Lord."

Romans 8:38-39

Birds of a Feather

I waited for you again friend
In the park, near the quiet end
Where we use to talk, you and I,
Laugh together, sometimes cry.
You said, you knew I'd be strong.
I thought you were never wrong.

Do you remember that day?
When together we both did say,
As we watched the birds fly overhead
At the same moment we both said,
Gazing at the sky: "Birds of a feather"
As they flew by, "flock together."

We laughed at what we heard
At the chorus of each word.
Now, I knew you wouldn't be there
But I looked for you today where
We used to talk and share—
And for a moment you were there

When I watched the birds fly by
And I thought, with a tearful eye
There's a promise in my heart
God will not forever keep us apart.
I will see you my dear friend,
We'll flock together once again.

> *"There's a promise in my heart. God will not forever keep us apart."*

We Went On Folding Laundry

I Wish

I wish that I could see you one more time.
I wish these words had power more than rhyme.

I wish that we could talk and laugh a while.
I wish that I could see your beautiful smile.

But Heaven's road is marked a one-way street,
And not until I too leave will we meet.

But still I find my heart cry once again.
I'll battle truth and longing 'til the end.

The truth that loved one, you will not come back.
And with longing, forward I must go to fill my lack.

It seems that Heaven could let you get away.
Could you be missed in eternity for a day?

But reason wrestles a battle with my heart.
Yes, yes, I knew the answer from the start.

So, when I see you, dear one, in heaven's eternity,
Oh run, oh run, straight, loved one, to me.

And smile the smile I've longed so long to see,
And know that God fulfilled a wish for me.

> *"So when I see you, dear one, in heaven's eternity . . . oh run, straight, loved one, to me."*

I Wish—Author's Reflection

And so we look forward to the glorious day when we see our loved ones again, our loved ones that have died in Christ Jesus. In John 11:25 Jesus stated clearly why we are not like those without hope. Jesus said, *"I am the resurrection and the life: he that believes in me, though he were dead, yet shall he live."* And our loved ones who sleep in Christ, who died before us, *yet shall they live.* And we will see that smile that we've longed so long to see and say too: *O, grave where is your victory?*

> *But I would not have you to be ignorant, brethren,*
> *concerning them which are asleep,*
> *that ye sorrow not even as others which have no hope.*
> *For if we believe that Jesus died and rose again,*
> *even so them also which sleep in Jesus*
> *will God bring with him.*
> *I Thessalonians 4:13-14*

> *I will ransom them from the power of the grave;*
> *I will redeem them from death:*
> *O death, I will be thy plague;*
> *O death, I will be thy destruction..*
> *Hosea 13:14a*

> *O death, where is*
> *thy sting?*
> *O grave, where is*
> *thy victory?*
> *I Corinthians 15:55*

We Went On Folding Laundry

Personal Reflection

Personal Reflection

Part IV

The Process of Grief— Collective

A time to mourn

Eccl. 3:1b,4b

Remembering Our Lady of Angel's School Fire

I was just a small child myself

when the story was told to me

Of the children who died in a school fire

in the city of my home and family.

Now it is the anniversary;

and many years have passed

Since the day of the searing fire,

the smoke and soot and ash.

It was part of my childhood memories

to think of those sad days;

It was the elementary school,

Our Lady of Angel's fire, the searing blaze.

There was a teenage boy in our neighborhood,

dark-haired, tall and thin,

Soon, he said, with a quiet seriousness,

his college years would begin.

He came by our home and told us

of something that had happened years before.

He told how he was in the Lady of Angel's fire

in the school on the second floor.

He said he was told to pray,

and when he was about to say a word

There was a voice within him,

> *"But Jesus said,*
> *Suffer little*
> *children, and*
> *forbid them not, to*
> *come to me:*
> *for of such is the*
> *kingdom of*
> *heaven."*
> *Matthew 19:14*

We Went On Folding Laundry

compelling him, and jump he heard,

Jump! So to the window he went
as thick smoke blackened the air,
And he jumped and landed painfully
on the concrete below him there.

Such courage this boy had—
both of his legs had been broken.
"But here I am today,"
he said gently and very soft spoken.

Because you could hear within his words:
I am here, but so many are not.
And yet, in his words you could also hear:
Those who are gone, no one forgot.

As a child I would go to bed at night
and start my prayers:
Now I lay me down to sleep,
and I'd mention my small woes and cares.

Maybe because I knew this story
that many school children have also been told,
I would ponder before my night's rest:
Would I rather die in a fire or of the freezing cold?

I then came to the firm conclusion,
I'd rather die in my sleep!

"As a child I would go to bed at night and start my prayers: Now I lay me down to sleep."

And so I'd continue my prayer:

I pray the Lord my soul to keep.

I have thought of those children who died,
even now after many years.
I've paid homage to them. Mentioning them,
I've seen eyes swell with tears.

As a teacher I would stand
in front of my classroom and say:
Because of the lives of this very special group
of children our lives are safer today.

Whether I was teaching in
an elementary school or a high school,
I spoke of this school fire and what was the benefit;
I spoke of it as a rule.

I always told my students on the day
of the fall fire drill, the Lady of Angel's story —
From something that was sad,
something good had come, something to their glory.

Perhaps it is too simple to say
that ninety-two children and three sisters died
For all the countless —because of increased fire prevention—
that later would be saved.

> *"I pray
> the Lord
> my soul
> to keep."*

We Went On Folding Laundry

They were saved because of all the improvements
in fire codes and rules.
This would make life safer and better
for generations of children in schools.

And we know God will not always give
reasons and everything explain.
But when we see Him face to face,
then everything will be very plain.

I think about the day of the fire and wonder:
What if our eyes could supernaturally see?
Certainly, we'd have seen the angels.
Yes, the angels of those children were busy, so busy.

Some said, "Dear Child, time to go home.
I'll walk you through the gate of eternity."
Others said, "Dear One, I'm just watching over you,
but you won't leave with me.

There are jobs to do, and some must continue on;
though some have finished here, too."
Like the tall thin neighborhood boy,
who was going to college, he knew.

He knew he had a job to do, as did the five children
from the fire who became firemen.
I'm sure there are many more stories

> *"God will not always give reasons and everything explain. But when we see Him face to face, then everything will be very plain."*

to be told like the stories of them.

And the Lady of Angel's fire changed lives
for people who were never there;
It made the world safer, more secure
for school children everywhere.

We do not seek it, but what is brought forth
after loss can be a gift when understood.
And we know the death of God's Son
brought about the world's highest good.

I thought: I would've liked to have seen
the playground of heaven that day
When ninety-two children with angels
and three nuns jumped on the swings to play.

What a contrast it was
compared to life on mournful earth.
On earth there was deep sorrow;
in heaven—joy, laughter, mirth.

Kneeling at my bedside I was taught to pray:
If I should die before I wake,
And then the most important words to say:
I pray the Lord my soul to take.

> *" ...what is brought forth after loss can be a gift when understood. And we know the death of God's Son brought about the world's highest good."*

We Went On Folding Laundry

It was hard to understand when my younger brother
died before he would wake one day.
Maybe he had prayed like me. Fire or cold?
No, in my sleep take me away.

But I have learned, those who are left behind here
when our loved ones leave,
There is no special way for our loved ones to depart
in which we will not grieve.

But I've decided I'll stick to my prayer:
Please take me when I'm sleeping somewhere.
Still there is a better prayer. We have often said it
with its deeper meaning unaware.

It is a prayer many have recited,
and it is a much more worthy one.
I'm sure at Lady of Angels they said:
Our Father who art in heaven…Thy will be done.

I continue to tell this story after a fire drill
to my students each year
About the young school children who
affected their lives who are no longer here.

Many are looking forward to seeing them,
and I'm looking forward to greeting
These children who grew up in our Father's house.

> *"…those who are left behind here when our loved ones leave, There is no special way for our loved ones to depart in which we will not grieve."*

It'll be an interesting meeting.

I'll tell them the difference they made,

but also of the sadness that was on many a face.

And they'll say, "Well, you must be glad to be here.

There's no sadness in this place."

The memory continues. It's been many long years

since the Lady of Angel's school blaze.

It made life safer. That's a legacy

that will last into eternity, and that's a lot of days.

Now we know why Christ said

in heaven are many mansions, many galore.

Because sometimes in one hour nearly one hundred children

can arrive at heaven's door.

The precious souls of God's children,

live with Him eternally, long after any fire's ash.

Of all that is tried by fire, the souls,

like precious jewels, silver and gold will last.

The loving memory continues and though

there still remains here on earth some pain,

Beauty from ashes is true! Our loved ones in Christ,

we shall be united with them again.

When I'm ready to fall asleep,

I still say my prayers at night.

We Went On Folding Laundry

> *"The precious souls of God's children, live with Him eternally, long after any fire's ash."*

The Memory Continues *(p.8 of 8)*
Remembering Our Lady of Angel's School Fire

When I think on this, I keep my eyes

on the true last picture of the Lady of Angel's sight.

As a child of God I envision the glorious mansions

and the playgrounds and more.

And I remember, God said for his children,

He has beyond our imagination more in store.

When I say my prayers, thinking of heaven

and casting upon Jesus all my care,

I trust in Jesus' word, He said:

"If I go, I go to prepare a place for you there."

If I don't wake up one morning, you can find me where,

ninety-two children were

Joyfully swinging with their angels and three nuns,

you can find me there.

The memory continues . . .

> *"… thinking of heaven and casting upon Jesus all my care,*
> *I trust in Jesus' word, He said:*
> *'If I go, I go to prepare a place for you there'."*

Remembering Firemen and the Heroes of 9-11

Well, I'm a fireman's daughter.

I'm proud of that; it's true.

My daddy put out fires

And saved many lives too.

I remember one Christmas day,

I asked my mom, putting presents by the tree,

"We're celebrating our Savior's birth today.

Why does Daddy have to be away from me?"

My mama looked me in the eyes and said,

"He's laying down his life for others to be saved.

Daddy's doing what our Savior did."

One time at church a man spoke to me

About firemen in a passing way.

"It seems they sit around; that's what I see.

What do firemen do all day?"

My Sunday school teacher smiling said, "I'll tell.

Yes, they wait, but when they hear the fire bell,

To save lives, they run straight into hell."

Well, I'm a fireman's daughter.

I'm proud of that; it's true.

My daddy put out fires

And saved many lives too.

Senior prom night, Mama said to me,

"This is something Daddy won't want to miss."

She drove me to the firehouse for Daddy to see.

We Went On Folding Laundry

Mama took a picture. Daddy gave me a kiss.

And my dad said, wearing his uniform of blue,

"Honey, you're beautiful. I'm so proud of you."

We waved goodbye, proud of my father too.

On 9-11 many brave firefighters died.

Into burning buildings they went, others to save.

For those who sacrificed their lives, I cried,

And for their families standing at a grave.

This fireman's daughter said, "For firemen I pray.

Greater love has no man than to give his life that way.

America's proud of its heroes who died that day."

Well, I'm a fireman's daughter.

I'm proud of that; it's true.

My daddy put out fires

And saved many lives too.

"Greater love has no man than to give his life that way.

America's proud of its heroes who died that day."

A Fireman's Daughter—Author's Reflection

The Bible is filled with the stories of many heroes: David against Goliath, Daniel in the lion's den, and the many men and women followers of Christ who were willing to be persecuted for their faith as spoken of in Hebrews, chapter eleven. There are still today those in the world who are persecuted for their faith in Christ. They are heroes for the faith. And yet heroes exist in our everyday life. On September 11, 2001, or 9-11, we saw these everyday heroes come out of the woodwork, and lay down their lives for their fellow men. Our troops , our military, continue to lay down their lives for us. And every day we find ordinary, selfless people willing to do the same. They are our heroes. Jesus said there is no greater love than this than to lay down your life for others. It is the greatest act of love.

Greater love hath no man than this, that a man
lay down his life for his friends.
John 15:13

And whosoever will be chief among you
let him be your servant.
Even as the Son of man came
not to be ministered unto,
but to minister; and
to give his life a ransom for many.
Matthew 20:27-28

The Empty Desk *(p.1 of 2)*
Remembering Andy and a special sixth grade class

It was Friday afternoon. Everyone was smiling; our work was complete.

Each student chattered happily, cleaning the room to make it neat.

There were twenty joyful voices. A three-day weekend was ahead.

Excitement sparked like electricity in what everyone did and said.

The world was lush and green in springtime; the school year neared the end.

After this long weekend, we'd come back for a few weeks and the conclusion.

Everyone mentioned all the fun things they intended to do.

Picnics were planned aplenty, and parties, visiting friends and relatives, too.

That's the story of how the long weekend did begin,

But it's a different story how the three days would end.

Three days later it was hard to understand when only nineteen of us would meet.

There were twenty of us on Friday, and now an empty seat.

Our hearts were heavy to see the empty desk in the front row.

We all felt our eyes burn as together we talked soft, sad and slow.

The pastor came into our classroom and said he would say a prayer,

As we all stared in silence at the empty, empty chair.

He said that our friend had once received God's greatest gift,

And as we prayed thinking of this, all of our spirits did lift.

As the day went on there were stories we would write and share,

And we put the empty desk in the middle of everyone there.

We all read our journals, and we cried and laughed at the words we had to say.

But we laughed best at the words our friend left behind in the journal to convey.

Teachers look out over their classrooms through the years,

And, yes, there are things that will bring them to tears;

And there is the laughter with the learning and many a funny moment.

Overall the experience is one of true fulfillment—

But today there was an empty desk. There were twenty of us on Friday.

Twenty would leave the classroom; nineteen would return. What to say?

Then there comes to mind a story, a story that is true.

The disciples stared and wondered at a place of emptiness, too.

There were twenty in the classroom on Friday; only nineteen would return.

There was a lesson scheduled on God's lesson plan for this class to learn.

There was long ago a Friday and three days later an empty tomb.

Now we had our Friday, and three days later an empty desk in our classroom.

And we know now, the lesson is from the greatest Book and the greatest story.

Oh death, where is your sting? Oh grave, where is your victory?

There are many empty places in life, but now an empty desk in this classroom.

Grave, where is your victory? Answer: It was swallowed up by an empty tomb.

Together we all wondered about heaven; it was so real now, but still so far away.

Is there sports? Pets? How many mansions can you run through in one day?

We were sure our friend would tell us smiling when we got there,

Beaming with pride, being the first one with the answer.

There were twenty on Friday and now, nineteen and an empty desk in our room,

And we found our comfort and hope knowing once there was an empty tomb.

When all the tests in life are over and the lights go out in the classroom,

There remains the final answer—

There is victory in death because of the empty tomb.

Bend Your Knee, Say a Prayer *(p.1 of 2)*
Remembering LCpl. James Bray Stack and our sacrificial military men and women

We love our troops.

We love these brave, gallant women and men.

We stand by them, courageous warriors.

We love our troops and remember them.

Our country started with every-day patriots

Minutemen who fought the battle well.

They knew the price of freedom took guts.

So today our country rings loud the liberty bell.

We love our troops.

We love these strong, valiant women and men.

We stand by them,daring warriors.

We love our troops and care for them.

We send our mighty troops our battles to fight,

Across roaring oceans to vast lonely lands.

They fight through difficulties, the dark of night.

These brave troops know war's demands.

We love our troops.

We love these sacrificing women and men.

We stand by them, honorable warriors.

We love our troops and hope for them.

We know the price is high for these brave souls,

But they know the price is higher if no one goes.

They lay their life down in dirty fox holes,

Bend Your Knee, Say a Prayer *(p.2 of 2)*
Remembering LCpl. James Bray Stack and our sacrificial military men and women

Or on a ship, a plane, or places only God knows.

We love our troops.

We love these heroic fighting women and men.

We stand by them, stalwart warriors.

We love our troops and pray for them.

So bend your knee, say a prayer, look on high tonight.

God holds a special place for them in heaven.

Our troops stand for freedom and what is right.

They give their life, the greatest gift that can be given.

We love our troops.

God bless our troops.

> *"We love our troops . . .*
>
> *So bend your knee, say a prayer, look on high tonight.*
>
> *God holds a special place for them in heaven."*

Heaven Knew This Man! *(p.1 of 2)*
Remembering President Ronald W. Reagan

America the beautiful was in mourning

And the world cried, too.

Rain poured down from the sky. Rain across the land.

The tears of heaven combined with the tears of man.

Heaven knew. Oh, heaven knew.

All earth and heaven together knew—

Heaven knew this man!

"Jesus wept."

John 11:35

America was not given a king,

But a common man to lead this land.

Though he was a common man, no common man was he.

He fulfilled a glorious God-given destiny.

And who would have imagined it would be so grand?

But heaven knew. Heaven knew truly.

Heaven truly knew this man!

America was blessed,

The home of the free and the brave,

When he came upon the stage of life to play a noble role.

He was everything good about America; he was a great soul.

This kind chief, a freedom fighter, the world salutes now in his grave.

Heaven knew this man for whom the forty church bells toll.

Heaven clearly knew this man!

America, a city upon a hill,

A beacon of light for all to see,

Shines brighter because of his great love for his homeland.

God blessed him with a First Lady of love who always held his hand.

America, America, God shed His grace on thee.

For heaven knew America needed this great man.

Heaven surely knew this man!

America, with eternal optimism

The Gipper would say, has not seen its finest hour.

But now there's sadness in the land of freedom's voice.

Yet at the moment of America's sorrow, the angels and God rejoice,

Welcoming he who represented the Sovereign's goodness and power,

Who now hears the words said: Well done, good and faithful servant.

This is your finest hour.

Oh, heaven knew! Heaven knew this man!

"Well done, good and faithful servant.

This is your finest hour."

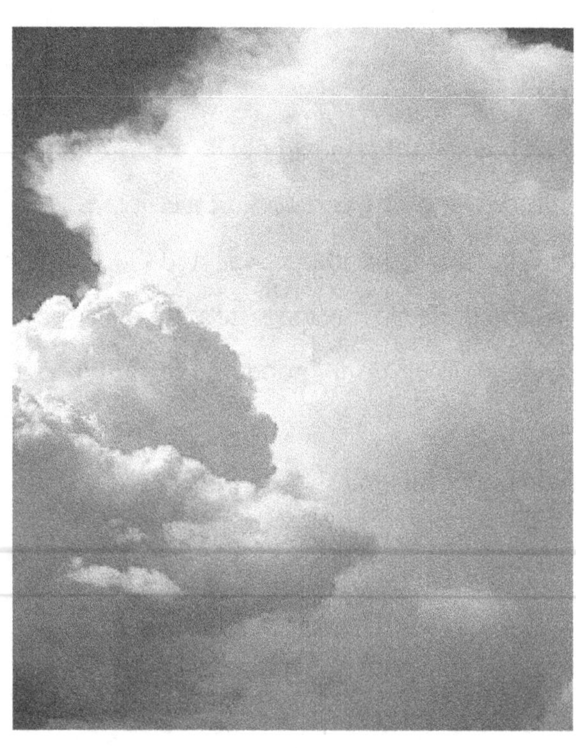

Personal Reflection

> *"Jesus said . . . I am the resurrection, and the life: he that believes in me, though he were dead, yet shall he live." John 11:25*

We Went On Folding Laundry

Personal Reflection

Part V

Eternal Life

A time to heal . . . to dance . . . peace.

Eccl. 3:3a, 4b, 8b

This is the promise that he has promised us... eternal life. I John 2:5

When All of Heaven Rejoices *(p.1 of 2)*

The birds on the telephone line listen each day,

Eavesdropping, you might say,

As the people talk and talk, day to day.

What do they say?

What does it sound like?

And the birds reply,

It sounds like idle chatter.

Most of the conversations hardly matter.

But when we hear a person say,

A baby was born—

What does it sound like?

It sounds like birds with youthful voices singing

Sweetly on an early spring morn

With the gentle peeping sounds

Of birds newly born.

And when we hear someone

On the telephone line say,

Someone committed their life

To Christ, our Lord, today—

What does it sound like?

It sounds like birds in green summer trees,

A joyful chorus singing

A beautiful melody, in harmony

With church bells ringing.

And we listen intently,

It is worthwhile

We Went On Folding Laundry

When we hear the news,
A child of God triumphed in a trial—
What does it sound like?
It sounds like birds with mature voices
In wind blown fall trees
Singing victoriously
Amidst gold leaves.

When we hear on the telephone line,
tears cried,
And someone says
One of God's children died—
What does it sound like?
It's as still as a midnight winter snowfall;

It's silent.
But that only lasts for a moment,
Then it turns into a riot.
It sounds like a loud parade and a band
Welcoming home a soldier from a faraway land;
It sounds like every bird on earth is singing
With a symphony and a chorus of angelic voices ringing.

What does it sound like?
It sounds like the birds
On the telephone line
Are a little closer to heaven,
And they know the times—when all of heaven rejoices!

> *" It sounds like the birds ... a little closer to heaven, ... they know the times— when all of heaven rejoices!"*

When All of Heaven Rejoices—Author's Reflection

There are many times to rejoice in life—but to realize at the time of our sadness of letting go of our loved one into Jesus' arms into eternity, is when all of heaven rejoices—to realize this is for some their greatest walk of faith, trusting in faith in the goodness of God and in the certainty of His promises. The contrast is earthly sorrow and heavenly joy. In heaven "it sounds like a loud parade and a band, welcoming home a soldier from a faraway land." Set against the contrast of our weeping, is the sound of heaven rejoicing when one of God's children arrives home in eternity. And the younger the person is who passes from this earth, the greater the challenge to accept that they left their life here, and instead will live their years that we expected them to be here on earth, in our home in Heaven. But for all ages, from the infant to the elderly, eternity is for God's children, a place, a heavenly home, and a person—our Savior Jesus, with outstretched loving, nail-scarred hands saying, amidst the heavenly rejoicing, *Welcome, my child, to the home I prepared for you with me in eternity— welcome to eternal life!*

Jesus said, In my Father's house are many mansions;
if it were not so, I would have told you;
for I go to prepare a place for you.
And if I go and prepare a place for you,
I will come again, and will receive you unto myself;
that where I am, [there] ye may be also.
John 14:2-3

But as it is written, Eye hath not seen, nor ear heard,
neither have entered into the heart of man,
the things which God hath prepared for them that love him.
I Cor. 2:9

Then Comes the Day of Singing!

Sarah, there is a song that you will sing in heaven someday.
I can hear it now, Sarah. You are singing; it is so sweet.
And I can see you, Sarah, dancing on a sun-drenched street
Of gold, shining gold. It is so real; it seems here today.

Sarah, there is a song you will sing in heaven, and I, too,
Will sing. I can hear it, Sarah! We are singing with glee.
Oh, Sarah, we are both singing, you and me so joyfully.
Many will share this song; a choir will sing with me and you.

Sarah, there is a song, and you are dancing to the melody.
I can see you dancing; how beautifully you move your feet.
It seems so near, Sarah—-this day we have to wait to greet,
This wondrous day of singing and dancing so beautifully.

Sarah, there is a song you will sing with the love you feel.
In your heart, the singing and dancing you already bring.
But the song I hear, Sarah—-the music that you will sing,
The song—-this song I hear is not here; yet it seems so real.

Oh, how you've waited, Sarah! You have waited many a year.
Then comes the Day of Singing! You throw away your cane.
No more crutch or walker, no more sorrow, no more pain.
It is not now, Sarah, dear songstress; yet in a blink, it is here.

The Painting of Paradise *(p.1 of 2)*

There is a place where heaven and earth meet.

The sky with soft white clouds and golden gentleness

Touches the green earth with warm tenderness.

And, oh, this place,

Our heart does gladly greet.

There is a place where the highest mountain peaks

Embrace the vast eternal sky of blue,

Growing on the mountains are forests of evergreen true.

With love, truth, and beauty,

To our hearts this speaks.

There is a place where the eagles fly in the majestic sky

Above the highest waterfalls and the rockiest seashore.

High above the clouds near heaven's open door.

There, our hearts, too, take flight,

Spread their wings and fly.

There is a place where wild flowers are growing.

We breathe the fragrant scent and see colors of teal,

Lavender, crimson and gold—heaven's palette they reveal.

This is the place we've longed for!

This our heart is knowing.

There is a place where the campfires are burning

In a safe wilderness with all the animals and the gentle deer.

There is warmth and cheer. There is no danger or fear.

We Went On Folding Laundry

The Painting of Paradise *(p.2 of 2)*

We are no stranger here.

This answers our heart's deep yearning.

There is a place we lose our desire to leave or to roam.

Our boat is tethered on the shore to a secure dock.

Windows glow with warmth; there's a door without a lock.

Every dusty pathway has led our feet here—

Our heart's home.

There is a place so beautiful—how can it in a painting be?

We can't imagine! The eye hasn't seen the coming glory.

But God granted this master artist, and us, to see

A little glimpse of the Master's painting of paradise—

Our home in eternity.

> *"Every dusty pathway has led our feet here—*
>
> *Our heart's home . . .*
>
> *Our home in eternity."*

Personal Reflection

"And this is the will of him that sent me,

that every one which sees the Son,

and believes on him, may have everlasting life."

John 6:40

Personal Reflection

We Went On Folding Laundry

And I heard a great voice out of heaven saying,

Behold, the tabernacle of God is with men, and he will dwell with them, and they shall be his

people, and God himself shall be with them, and be their God. And God shall wipe away all

tears from their eyes; and there shall be no more death, neither sorrow, nor crying,

neither shall there be any more pain: for the former things are passed away

And he that sat upon the throne said, Behold, I make all things new.

And he said unto me,

Write: for these words are true and faithful. Rev. 21:3-5

We Went On Folding Laundry

Author's Afterword

About the Dedication . . .

While writing this book, I sent a copy of the poem "Heaven Knew This Man!" to former First Lady, Nancy Reagan. The occasion for sending the poem was President Ronald Reagan's 100th birthday. Months passed and I received a letter apologizing for the time it took to get back to me, but acknowledging with gratefulness the poem about her husband. Since the book's dedication is for those who *continue on* after the loss of their loved one, then certainly our former First Lady's name could be added there, too.

And there is another name—and it is not that her name "could be" added there, but it was added on the *Dedication* page. The name is Ellen. Ellen was added, not because she *continued on*, but because she left us. On the day I finished writing the first draft of this book, I received a phone call telling me my sister-in-law, Ellen, had been struck by a car and killed crossing the road to get her mail.

Grief comes to all—the famous and the unknown. It comes to visit at the shoreline of everyone's life regardless of political party or station in life. But, Christ Jesus comes to all, too. All who will call upon His name, He will bring to them His spirit of gentle comfort and infinite love.

This book is dedicated to those who *continue on* after the loss of a loved one, but wrapped up in that package is the great love we have for those who left us. If that love had not been so great, there would be no trial to face to *continue on.* But love continues on. We went on folding laundry because that's what love would do.

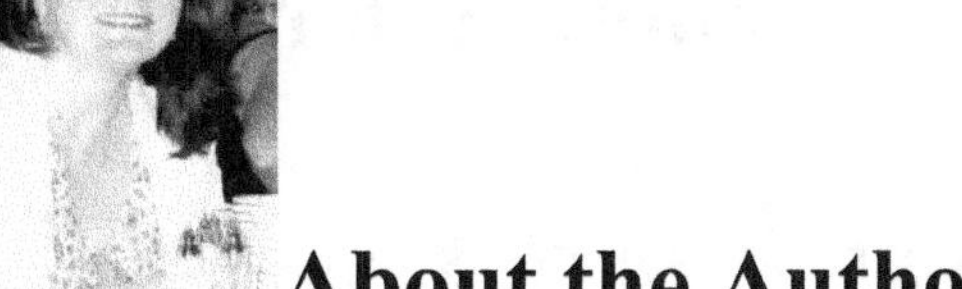# About the Author

Audrey Marie Hessler, a grief counselor in the Grief Share ministry for many years, and a teacher, speaker, author, and a poet, has written, *They Call Him Immanuel, God With Us, a Christian Poetry Devotional,* and *Lessons I've Learned as a Teacher.* A contributor to the series, *Refined by Fire,* and the devotional, *Daily Devotions for Writer,* her stories and poems have been published by Christian Liberty Press along with articles in other venues, recently published, a play for children, " *'Shhh!' Said the Trees".*

Contact Information

Contact the author at audreymarieinspirations@yahoo.com, or to learn more about her speaking ministry visit her website: **AudreyMarieHessler.com**

Purchase Information

We Went on Folding Laundry is available at Amazon.com, through bookstores, and may be purchased directly from the author.